Seasons

SEASONS

Sounds and Amorous Observations

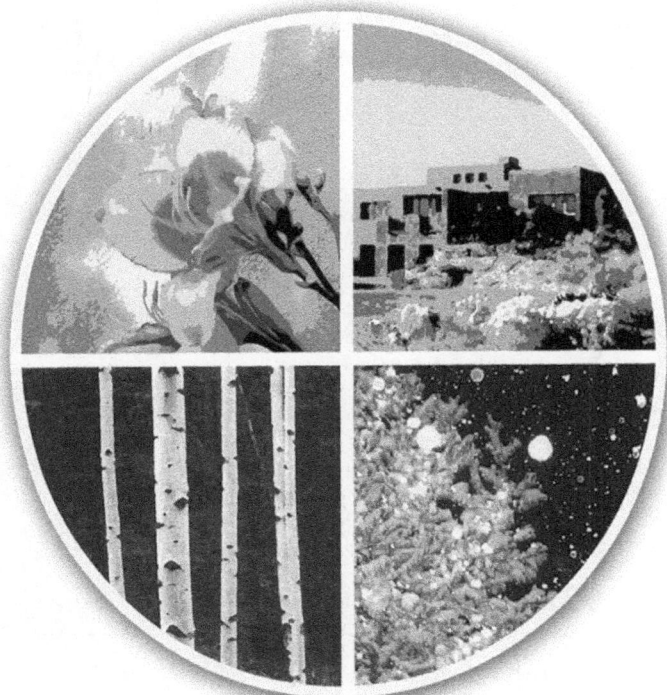

Poems

Andres C. Salazar

SUNSTONE
PRESS

SANTA FE

Sunstone books may be purchased for educational, business, or sales promotional use.
For information please write: Special Markets Department, Sunstone Press,
P.O. Box 2321, Santa Fe, New Mexico 87504-2321.

Cover design › James D. Patrick
Book design › Vicki Ahl
Body typeface › Poliphilus MT Pro
Printed on acid-free paper
∞

Library of Congress Cataloging-in-Publication Data

Salazar, Andres C., 1942-
  [Poems. Selections]
Seasons Sounds and Amorous Observations : Poems / By Andres C. Salazar.
  pages cm
ISBN 978-0-86534-969-8 (softcover : alk. paper)
I. Title.
PS3619.A433S43 2013
811'.6--dc23
                          2013030770

WWW.SUNSTONEPRESS.COM
SUNSTONE PRESS / POST OFFICE BOX 2321 / SANTA FE, NM 87504-2321 /USA
(505) 988-4418 / ORDERS ONLY (800) 243-5644 / FAX (505) 988-1025

Dedication

To the girls and women of my life—

Jean, Julie, Melissa, Justine, Kianna & Elisa

Contents

Season of Autumn ___ 81

Season of Winter ____ 109

Prologue

Poetic sounds of love included in this volume trace
themselves from youthful ardor to mature sadness, from a frightening
madness to a pensive pall, and like seasons, from spring-like hope to
one of wintry despair. Love takes us all from one level of passion
to another, driving us to say and do things that are irrational
and, upon reflection, we often deny that we ever said
or did them, possibly because they bare the soul.

The poems follow the author's observations while experiencing the force inside that makes us search for a soulful match with another person, one in which the feelings of infatuation, admiration and spiritual attraction emerge in many dimensions with vigor and persistence. The search sometimes takes us through several ventures but then we mature and learn the vicissitudes of the force as it manifests itself in real life, not in our imagination. The personal experience in the search can be wondrous if we do not let our ego mandate that feelings be reciprocal every time we sense the force at work. As in any search, there are places, times, situations that look promising but we must accept that there is no match and we must move on. This is not to say that the expended effort is small and the search easy to execute. On the contrary, the journey can be long and we can fall prey to settling for less than complete fulfillment. Recognizing that we have not reached our goal of a soulful match in such a person, we can still enjoy the company of such people and call the association what it really is – friendship – an interaction that enriches our lives and contributes to societal conformity. Hence, we can develop many friends, each providing a unique relationship which energizes us and yields at the same time, paradoxically, a welcome comfort and solace in our dealing with tribulations as well as crises in our lives. But a friend is short of a soulful match; the gap in affection is at least an order of magnitude. The difference is perhaps smaller for a son, daughter or blood relative depending on the bonding that a family relationship can bring, albeit restrictive due to cultural prohibitions.

To dwell on the physical aspects of love—the magnetic qualities of attraction, the corporeal aspects of looks, scent and touch, the sexual union—simply ignores its deeper, longer lasting, worldly and spiritually unique qualities like trust, respect, benevolence and generosity. Love over time allows these more admirable human traits to fully blossom in the relationship with the targeted companion, perhaps even spilling over into more general terms for those around us. But there is no denying that the physical interaction between two unrelated people plays an important role in the ultimate comfort and permanent companionship we seek, let alone the procreation that nature intended. The stimulation realized in the simple touch, embrace or kiss is universal and powerful beyond description. I believe this easily ignitable physical stage is the common element we have with the animal kingdom and the fact that we can control the urges of nature differentiates us as human beings and allows for a much deeper affection between two people. It is the supreme quality of our mind, the gift of reason we are bestowed and the result of our evolution, that permit us to dedicate and then channel our attention to the rare soul mate we seek before or after experiencing the fleeting pleasure of carnal knowledge. What starts out as a hormonal volcano in youth transitions to various strands of a human relationship and interpersonal feelings modulated by troubles sometimes caused by us and sometimes not. It is again our spiritual nature that allows us to continue the unshakeable relationship with the soul mate despite the interference wrought by these troubles. Time makes a difference in the relationship. Trust, fondness and respect grow and their roots become deeper.

Is there only one soul mate for us in the whole world? I believe there can be several people each of whom could become one's soul mate. We do not meet all of them and, except for a few people we choose to associate with, we do not have the time to develop the relationship to the extent we need to determine whether they are legitimate candidates or not. We are living in a hurried life today and this can lead to unhappy relationships. Too often we make commitments that we cannot keep with people we barely know. Too often we let our physical urges dictate our decisions. Too often we believe we have run out of time as in musical chairs. Love rarely grows from convenience and it is not nurtured by carnal gratification. The spiritual union between two people can overcome a lot of bumps in the road but that bonding requires a soul searching not all of us are willing to do. Such revelation goes far beyond taking your clothes off or letting your hair down which, for some people, is frightening enough. It puts in play a vulnerability that displays what we are truly made out of, what we truly believe, what we really want and why we want it. Our soul mate is the only person we trust with those priceless valuables of our life.

There are many ways in which the feelings of love can be expressed besides those of a physical nature. With the power of speech and accompanying body language, our minds can conjure up a myriad of amorous messages and nondescript sounds. Literature is rife with attempts to articulate these feelings, leaving in their wake a vocabulary and linguistic structure as rich as any earthly language. This idiomatic side of love can be simple as nature intended but also as complex as the human psyche can make it. The sounds of love from spoken or written lines can be funny or sad, personal or abstract, broad and metaphysical or specific and petty. Love generates images and fantasies that transcend language and so attempts to articulate what is happening can result in lines that are blurry or disconnected, even violating the linguistic or cultural rules of any human dialect. What is certain in the actual expression of love is that an irrepressible urge is there, that the connection is best when it is mutual, that time and duty are constantly getting in the way, and finally that hope for true fulfillment is forever burning until death. There is no substitute for love; as human beings we are blessed because we can write about it and make sounds about it, albeit imperfectly

Andres C. Salazar
Santa Fe, New Mexico
Spring 2013

Season
of
Spring

Endless Love

May I suggest an endless love,
No unsettled thoughts
In cool of woods, and
Supreme unction by the sun
Driving far the demons of unrest
Who spawn the lack of grace
And absence of alluring arms?

May I stroke your hair
And hold you in cream summers
And touch your genial breasts,
A reach for moistened lips
Making known to me a quiet bond?

Does there exist a longer day,
A tighter closing of the eyes
Made in life's sincerity
To let me stay
In wind and light
And serve you evermore?

So Mortals We Can Be

Let's tame the ardor passably
So mortals we can be
And live on earth as days go by.

We can hide our nakedness
And live within the lover's plight
Quarreling anxiously.
Can we live in time arranged
Where anger comes from words
Spoken impatiently,
From the mind and not the heart?
Insipid trials will test our souls
To find the depth of peace
All of us do seek.

Is There A Temper

Is there a temper for this youth
That gropes to find a mate
Without pain
But sends a heart to ecstasy?

Is there no path
To temple of pleasure
That evades the turmoil
Bending life to deal with truth?

A Niche of Quietude

Might I want you young, demure
With skin that rivals purity,
Perfect hands and feet
In golden springtime morns,
The scent of sunrise dew
And dreams of opened arms.

This, or nothing more
A niche of quietude
Amid a torrent of modern blare,
Listless summers,
Rage and insipid talk,

I find that opposites
Prolong the joy of having you
Even if the hour is short
And tired eyes behold you now.

How Far Is It?

How far is it to the heart of Eve
Her mystery and green eyes
Her lips to mine and fair
And feelings done and shared?

How far is it to the things that count,
The kingdoms of her hair
And splendor view of face
Her voice speaking only of our souls?

How far is it to the wherewith of her
Wherein lies her gathered cares
Behind walls she puts to me
Done to test and homage bring?

How far is it to the dawn of Eve
Her spirit, deep and drawn again,
Her hands, far and away from me,
As distant as they were before?

A Wish To Walk With You

A cloud of absence
Enwraps my days, tendering
A wish to walk with you
As we did that night
Through dark of incense,
Outside steamed up windows,
Looking into midnight parlors
When we saw and wondered at
A floury pizza master with
Cycle boots and incandescent eyes.

I remember the dampened chill,
My yearning for the time to slow,
A wish for yesteryear's candied joy,
A pair carving out initials again
Scoring truth on the lamppost's serenity.

A Murmur Of A Secret

A murmur of a secret
Passing from heart to lips,
A madness cooled by
The casual grant of kisses
Stopped only by angry time,
Conjures up the promise
You will keep at bay
Uncertain anguish
In shortness of the breath
Each passing day gives to me.

The Dream Is For Us To Wander

There is a place for birds
To sing full throated songs,
Their mirth mingling with the scent
That beguiles the lover close
For carpet upon a forest glen.

The morning sun streams through
The prism of the pillared branches
As they sway with melodious breeze
The lustrous dew becoming mist
It plays its part in luring youth.

The dream is for us to wander
Upon a view to count the ways
We can lose ourselves to bliss
Our breath becomes but one
Expressing strongly our consent.

Come To Me Before The Time

I need you in the meantime
Between the years and say
The days and between the while,
In the during during
Eternally, farther than the always,
Deeper than the now.

Come to me before the time
The half past then
Where the sky meets the far
Timeless in the when
Awhile in forever,
Pausing and a star.

Embrace me for the meet,
And interlude of books
Passing the span of twice
Close to me and age
Absolutely and without size.

Kiss me before your busy
In spite of the near
And closing under
When the moon greets the in,
Seasons of the infinite,
Amid cycling love's begin.

The Wordless Walks and Grass

Come with me and covet
All the please and tender,
Holding moments in the air,
Surrendering your green eyes to me,
To bring the here and glow
To the always sweet embrace.

Come with me and share
The wordless walks and grass
Soothing hills and singing seas,
Lively brooks and lifted boughs
Making music beside your face
To swaying trees all in bow.

Come with me and stay
The old and days of years
Waving them to slide above
Our mount of lure and life,
Causing then the lovers' time
To be ten to ten and then again.

How Kind It Is To Muse

Sometimes I think of the dress
You wore
Your gathered hair,
Its silken strands of brown
And how you looked afar
And gave me whisperous grace.
How kind it is to muse
How deep the days will be
And intent to welcome charms,
Warming with their suns
Our arms
In long embrace.

Far, Immense To Passion

Your hand to chin, a pensive couch
Radiantly finding ways
To please what has moved.

Far, immense to passion
In silence, feeling the hours left
Before I cross again and share
The dreamt and days
Softly thought by you today.

Harkened there, beckened comes
The forbidden look
To ask what unforgiving joy
She renders next to me.
Comes anew her smile,
The thought was broken
Left tossed hair, a hand caressing it
The joy did come.

Recover, The Night Is Still

A song of spring lifts travail
Over fragments of mistaken past
A new life, vibrant, primed
Intense to fall the more
Or garrison of love receive.

Sultry dreams convince
The trembling hours to let
And semblance of comfort bring;
Gloriously warm breath
Kindling hopes still comes the one
Innocent, fondling the wounded slip.

Recover, the night is still, patient,
Holding yet the thoughts
Tenderly planning for tomorrow's kiss
Secretly, for days that never end.

Songs Autumnal Ask

Songs autumnal ask
Our hope regain
Replenish memories,
Holidays the meadow's gift
Bearing a kiss of winter
Shared, foregone the future cares.

These songs and cries
The orb of time be stopped
Amidst delay to rapture
And hear you sigh
Savoring from a moment ours
An embrace of small eternity.

A Humming Of Temples

Your head slides away into fancy,
The arms holding me
Eyes escaping to a misty fog,
Lips with moistened invite
A growing pressure
Consecrated by the stars
And light on this hill of frankincense.

As I draw nearer
A warm ether surrounding,
Our bodies now in perfection, a breast pliant as roses
Or honey—colored throat
Slipping away into fantasy,
Throbbing for ancient service,
We drift into a humming of temples,
The law becomes a union of hearts.

Autumn Leaves In Spin

She is the gleam of spring
Sprinkled in evening bloom,
Clouds in sunny glare,
All that life can bring
And blare of rain and ice,
Her eyes dispelling any hovering gloom.

She is the place of fervent spring
Sung in shadows of the two,
Autumn leaves in spin
And thoughts remembering
The kisses she'll give to me,
Threads running slowly in lover's loom.

A Huarache Walk

A huarache walk in Asbury Park
With swarms of walkers,
Yearned for somewhere else.
A coolside breeze on boardwalk sands
Gave us mounts of flesh
And the hairy, molded lips
Of Moloch and Mammon twins,

But with the din behind us
Facing the ocean's foam and spray,
A quiver of its heart played to me
The happiness of your waist
And music of your hair.

We'd Never Have To Speak Again

For each word we've heard and said
I'd like to kiss you two
For only then would words say too
The way I've wished instead.
We'd never have to speak again
Just care and hold aloft
Our times together
Taken slowly, outside in gentle rain.

Nightly Breezes And A Star

Nightly breezes and a star,
Quiet lands afar and green
Freshly done with evening dew,
There is an image of precious care.

Your laugh and hands adrift
Dancing with a partner's flair
I see myself coming there
Sharing such a sight with you.

Sewn together in long embrace,
Tenderness in the air
Your face radiates the joy we make
I cannot stop for destiny.

When Hearts Finally Meet

I heard a murmur passing by
That chills the promise I did seek
About the madness we could make
Together, after dark tonight.

The secret is that rumor
Grows the yearning even more
When hearts finally meet
And pledge ourselves to keep.

Not too soon you came
My breath did stop
My hand in yours
Your smile did beckon me.

I remember not the play
Nor route that took us there
A moonlit place beside a bridge
Some nightly birds for company.

There were no words that spoke
Of ecstasy nor sounds of glee
We simply were too glad
Of our union through the night.

Mountain Of Myrrh

I will go to the mountain of myrrh;
She lives there and waits for me,
Storing blue of sky and evening fun,
The rain she catches apron full,
Gathering freshness of the sun,
She carefully tends the bed of April cool.

I will go to the mountain of myrrh;
Every step my heart does feel,
The wait worth every pain,
She sings my dreams aloft,
Brooks echoing them again,
Trees in envy provide a melody soft.

I will go to the mountain of myrrh;
Stirs the regard for me,
Her face will be next to mine,
Already her eyes draw me near,
Her aura a welcome sign,
She too has waited for this moment dear.

It Was A Moment's Passion

Steamed windows let us know
It was a moment's passion
That stole us from our books
And focused reason,
Far away to wrinkled dreams,
Elbows getting in the way.

We pushed away our mental ties
And wrapped ourselves until the end
When the steering wheel became
Too hard to work around
Despite our warmth too far
And shoes that had been shed.

We had kissed too long,
The night had raced our hearts
And ardor began to cool
It was time to let you go,
Dorm gates were about to close
My sleepless night awaited me.

I Failed To Calm My Soul

I failed to calm my soul
When the hour was nearly here
It went about its random way
Like a spirit seeking sense.
And though my eyes were closed
I could see you coming near
Quietly, at the close of day.
There was this rush inside
A boundless force compelled,
The scent of zeal gave sight
There was only scant to say
Your face had given light
In such a darkened day.

Season
of
Summer

She Said My Words Are Paper

She said my words are paper
Useful, only
To light up her whims and cigarettes
She smokes between the maybe's
Passed when reading magazines.

She said my search was paper
Useful, only
When cutting time was here
Or reading to laugh the tears away
Brought about by daily whims
When they start to sting.

She said "my words are make believe,
One's private life
To paper cannot be penned
And said and measured there
Because 'it's unclear'
What I mean and say and do
And versify sometimes."

She said paper pieces
Were not from her
Or even the sometimes her
Because it's hard to look
At things as lines demand.
Rather it's best
To write the quick
Not knowing what form it takes.

I Like You In Your Trivia

I like you in your trivia,
Dime colognes, fashion seconds,
Chartreuse, and would be colors,
Chewing gum, romance comics
All the more in skin and hair
And unwinking eyes
For what I like are not
In public beauty or momentary praise.

She's my wish in washed and disheveled hair,
Blemished by her weakness,
Imperfect as the world
Whose glory is in the smallest things.

Parting

I dreamt the pain did come,
She said I—have—to—go.
I felt the loss and rush to say
What cease of cycle I can make.
But reddened change did prevail
And swift her words did collapse
My dreamlike worlds of her with me.

The words still ring the terror of yesterday
A ghostly figure gone and far;
The nights are days and endless hours
Changing nothing in my gloom.

I sense the fear and score
Of tortured waiting amidst a grayish fog
That lingers like unanswered prayers.

But She Is Sad and Far

I've fallen into the deadly state,
Weak and limber and shyly done,
Linked to her and gone to see
How might I mark the date
When nearness we could share
Unfolding then the aura of the mind.

I wait for her to take me in
And keep my fate and gentle path.
She's one with spirit felt in woods,
When winds stir the sleeping leaf,
I dream deeply of idyllic walks,
All the songs we might make,
But she is sad and far;
She does not answer and bequeath
The hours we'll spend in certainty.

Past September, May and June,
The chill of night in mid November
Winter and all of spring
And many years of roaming aimlessly
Lost of age and sweet remember
Of all the growth together,
And bloom we missed in youth.

She's There In The Grocery Store

She's there in the grocery store
Choosing cans for me,
Her hair sweetly combed
And smiling at our bread.
She heaps potatoes
And looks at me. I adore her now
In fragrance of the fruits,
Plucking oranges, two or three.

Her green eyes choose the meat,
Shakes her head at milk and cheese,
Our meals become our daily words,
More nourishing with each passing day.
Her cotton dress makes her seen
The best of all. Too large and cheaply made,
It shouts at me in many ways,
She's my soul and not a goddess in disguise.

Don't Smile At Me

Don't smile at me and softly touch my hand
If loving words are all you want from me.
I cannot be a playful box of words
Or sweet reminders slowly sent to you.
Your smile sends me in violent speed
Toward a point I cannot reach,
Of owning you and becoming me.

Don't smile at me and speak softly
If friendly talk is all you seek.
No few moments of tender words,
Will satisfy my quest for more,
More than time of talk and sweet polite
I have a thirst for eternity.

Don't smile at me and pat me one more time,
I cannot answer gently and control the sound
From my soul that stirs for more,
Gorging then the moments given me.
Do not touch me as it may be lasting,
The action that my heart will take.

Don't smile at me with soulful glance,
I cannot saunter quietly and speak poetic pause
Wasting days when I yearn for more,
Sealing bonds that nature cannot break.
I sense a relentless fear building up,
Unleashing then a rage to fill the need.

Mary With Guitar

Mary with guitar,
Warmth from sundown
Sending her to play
Softly, in the tired afternoon.

Mary with guitar,
Shades of amber
Sitting on the floor
Alone, in the peaked afternoon.

Lingering thoughts misplay
The music pizzicato
The past is heavy
And shrieks a—blast
Superrupt
Mary with guitar.

It Is Too Late

The river brought us life
And we drank our joy from it,
Waiting for the Russian Olive scent
To shake us from a dream.

I remember walking home
Your hand in mine,
The stars were young,
My body vibrant, radiant
From their pulsing light.

Was there a garden for us?
Aglow with nature's gifts
That the gods arranged
And we had strayed too far
The memory becoming clear
It bespeaks of agony?

And you were born
In other rooms, in olden times,
The magic is not ours,
For a promise must be kept.

Darkly, a chill is felt
And the dawn never comes
To see the freshness
Flower in your hair.
And to hear your laughter
Wander through the yawning space.

As A Pebble In A Stream

Black on white artfully done
To tease a man
Out of an abstract existence
Technically obscuring an inner life.

Powerful is a wisp of feeling,
An irrepressible thought,
An imagined caress,
The sense betraying time and
The foggy terrain where I live.

Still you come, unsure
As a pebble in a stream,
Waters from melting snow,
A winter almost behind us.
Tomorrow, what our lives?

How Foolish Rain Does Seem

How foolish rain does seem
This wintry day distraught,
Intent towards saddening
A parasol of pristine giggles
And impudent happiness
In rubbing our hands
Somehow finding delights aboard.

The icy storm falls upon us
As it does upon the delicate life.

Aubade In Wet December Jersey

Aubade in wet December Jersey
Smokewashed shores tired,
As from Leander's stroke,
The song falters
In a Pennsy station;
Even thinking of you
Does not make the anthill
Cease its stir,
Its option to drown
A memory of desire's minim
Last night in wake
Of an inglorious day
A debenture and note
Of human feelings,
A touch of gentle warmth
In a jostling gigapolis.

A Banana Bread Night

A banana bread night
Couched on a broad shouldered carpet
Whispered rudely
Facing desires uncommonly lain
After a glutton's pizza.

And peppers strengthened
Our rush to irrational lips,
A gentleness swallowed,
A meaningfully bitter lemon
And fragrant hair.

An enormity of softness
Fed by an ache to touch
Surrendering without question
Fails the night, trembling
At the strangeness, a no
Sprouted by the disease of fear.

A Taste Of Seizure

Asunder desire tears life,
Changing where there was order,
Violently spills the need
For the clasp to last forever
A touch tingling into time.
The fire, a taste of seizure
Inspiring this gift called now.
She moves gently
To please demands of feeling
Beyond mortal chambers.
Instantly, instantly
The pressure returns,
An aim towards light implicit
And capture of an insatiable wish
Now with miscast looks
Strewn when blinded by a force
Spelled slowly in royal garb
Of human frailty.

A Bid To Leave

It was not a misspoken word
Nor ill—tempered wind
That drew a silence.

Nor was it then a feature
Found in someone else
With wish for newer laughter
And kinder hand or fair.

Silently, it was a stillness
Of the face and arms,
Words never heard before
And eyes that ask
What time it is,
A bid to leave
And close of doors
Which lead to a
Darkness of the lost.

Fallen From The Fear Of Time

The ancient door opens,
A stream of light let into shadows
Left over in quiet repose
From a galaxy of tears
Fallen from the fear of time.

It does not matter now,
Our choice for this bond,
Find our bodies draped
By regal—colored ardor
And silent communion.

Beside me now a silhouette
Stirring from a flight
Of mountains moving in the past,
Streaks of memories dubious
Waiting only for the mortal wish
Now committed, now secured
By the strange sensation
All becoming somehow unknown.

From A Meeting With Adversity

Quietly in the countryside
On meadowed earth and life
I think of mornings
Spent with you
When I was ill
My life belonging to despair
And alone your presence
Lifted my dismay
And a sun did traverse
Its misconcerted path to me
Surging energy
As it covers me anew
With fears and blindness
From a meeting with adversity
Lingering as an ill.

July Fourth

The trees lay against the sky
Cloud—steeped gathering bed
Brushing past aged time.

Your hands symboled answers
To caress and long embrace
Promising to receive anew
This grass—laden moment
Beckoning nature's ardor now.

Thundering forests
And tender lobes of the earth
Speak the timeless thought
Quieting the sadness
The hours do pass
Duress implicit
Hovering over us
Even now in touching arms.

A Winter Lies Beyond

A fall remonstrate
The passing days,
Young, alive and mystery
The delight of first meetings
And jubilant, freshened spring.

Far into dark seasons
Burns the endless wish
Aims to crave you more
A hunger filled someday
With secrets we will share.

A winter lies beyond
A waiting, ambered kiss,
A welcome to the eyes
Whose depth contain
A quieter shade of life.

Miles Are Strands Of Time

Miles are strands of time
Placed there to test
The worth of man
And strength of gift
Gloriously sent in swoon
And honor of your manner,
A likeness to a separate beauty,
Human like in flaws,
Distinctive in due measure
Of perilous charms and things,
A brazen calyx poised for service
Or a hand shown in peace.

Asbury Park

To remember the rolling of moons,
How we spoke between the sounds
Of pixelated winds
Stepping on the sands
And wretched tears of ocean
Seen as lonely in the summer.

Planks on the boardwalk
Were our feet
Running for miles
As they strained
To nimbly reach infinity.

I held your hand,
Still cold from uncertain yearning
As a taste of salty wave
Having leaped to our lips,
Witness to our glance.

How many days are there?
Remembered hard,
How many tides
Before this small laughter
Can be ours to keep?

Reaching Out For Heaven

The wind blends the grains of time,
My eyes stinging in remembrance
Of irreverent moments without you,
Less the honor of your hair
Or the fragrant blossoms
tossing heads in glee.

Merge the tissues, together fire,
The pledge akin to staff of wheat
Reaching out for heaven,
The touch of stars a pinnacle
Finally glad to simply penetrate
The blue clarity of skies,
Undulating from Aeolus,
His breath as strong
As our bonds to human happiness.

A Child From Our Window

Imagine fields and quiet songs,
The sun and water dancing in our veins
And in a distance fair
A flux of joy among the trees,
A child from our window
His cheeks reddened by our strength,
A gentle miracle in our consort.

This honed with all the pain
And the anger—flushed impatience
We can with tenderness
Cultured with a pair's endearment
Quell discomfort in his eyes
Opened only with our rage to live
And hunger for relief.

Slowly, with fields and songs benign
The dusk and death we learn from him.

In A Wake Of Routine Living

Nightly gloom of absence,
Waiting for a Tuesday glimpse
Shorn from your timely magic,
A pause and breathless meeting,
Frantic heart's hopeless garbled mouth.

In a wake of routine living
Somehow we miss the hope
And quiet face of love...
And deal with jagged edges
Of inane distraught,
Plainly life, words
We do not wish to hear.

On goes the sadness,
The human pride
Resplendent in its conquest
Of a fool's desire for you.

You Are Coming Near

Cruel sounds fill the hours
As the day wanders through a
Stealthy past——
An unjust number of insulting things
A darkened thought
Somehow suggested a long time ago
Foreboding and now comes to haunt
A wish to be alone, and to be
Stretching out into existence again
Feeling that the self is here to grieve.

And how these dismal airs pass
When there is a hint
You are coming near,
Ready and appear
Although you are tired
But you will give
As our nature always does
To an endless fantasy.

The World Now In Concert

A night engages the need for arms
Two moments held in time
Through a kiss, a careless lock,
A smile from the hardened past,
All seen now
And approximate a youthful joy
Lost somewhere in walks of tedium.

A floating hand, the soundless rhythm
Of yearning for a touch of life
A desire exchanged
As secrets pass between the lips,
The eyes have sent a bid;
The world now in concert,
Excitement
Smooth as adagio encores
Remembered on a cool summer night.

The identity of life is lost
As surrender nears;
An impelling dimlit room
Will harbor now our souls...

A Separate Grace

A separate grace comforts me
Serenading long forgotten songs
With slightly tilted head
A quiet look thrown along
Forward, bound to arms
A desire to hold forever
This tread to meet.

We come together
In this awkward night
Braving the noise of rain
The coldness of an earth.

We warm our hands
Cupped to keep the warmth
From fleeing
To a darkened world
Bent to misunderstand.

How Quiet The Gods Do Seem

Together in a summer twilight
Remembering branch laden blooms,
As shadows wrap themselves
And chirps become louder still.

You speak and mark when
A meandering breeze did stop
And measured heartbeats
To our presence on the field.

And the moments still to come
Of sharing comfort in this dark
To keep the fears away
From dimming then the stars.

How quiet the gods do seem
This night refrained from glare
And their monitor
And cups of bitters
Taken well some time ago.

Ash Wednesday

We met in the winter and Ash Wednesday,
The world outside to us.
We laughed at our silly selves
And embraced to keep the dark away.

The day was bleak and the future worse
With our hands we gathered strength
To keep at bay the wrongs
And stopped to dry the tears.

I kissed her then and then again
Trying to forget the wretched fears
Deadly ones taken in a chance
And fancies taken in the spring.

But now in winter is desire
With glowing embers strong and amber
Rekindling ever
All the fires of yesteryear.

I Walked Into A Cloud

I walked into a cloud
Stretching arms into the mist
Turning round to touch someone,
Also seeking partner fair.

A quiet tune did have me sway
Again, something drew me near
I felt someone there in play
Moving, waiting for me dear.

They told me later
I had walked into a wall
Where senses leave a mark
How thin the wish became.

Waking finally from the dream
To salve the wound it made
And how real it made it seem
Hoping now the ache will fade.

Irresistible

You came out irresistible
Plaid skirt, gray and green
With dark blue sweater,
Turtle neck,
Green corduroy light jacket,
Large, black rimmed sunglasses
Red rinsed hair, neck—length
Carefully combed,
Beautifully full legs,
Now newly sheen of roséd
Stockings,
Thin perfectly formed
Lips, pale red lipstick,
Framing glistening white
Teeth and smile.

Because Your Eyes

Because your eyes are those of Beatrice
Adored by me and more
Without these lines and all the rest
Without the world and all of sleep.

Because your eyes are those I want to see
Far beyond the ones of time
I want to kiss you farther now
Than pressing lips for moment's sake.

Because your eyes are green and sad
I want to hold you now and deep
Keeping all my warmth for you
In worlds cold and cloudy skies.

Because your eyes are green and far
This longing is for naught
You'll never come, I know that now,
These lines I write for heartfelt lies.

Sounds Of Meek And Boredom Flow

I am weak because of Eve
And always in the fool
When she's near and I speak,
Sounds of meek and boredom flow.

It's all a child's play for her
Amusing her the garbled words.
She plays with me in all my plain,
My approach made coarse.
Troubling yen has filled my mind
I forget to see and sense does flee.

Less ardor may win her view
But instead of dying, the throb goes on.
In disarray I'll lose her now,
There go my hopes for joyful sun.

Leading Back To Control

Leading back to control
Forsaking instincts inbred to yield
To gentlest course
An homage to gravity
And human form possessed.

Resounds the well pithed mouth,
Age—old in honor, protection
Of the incumbent jewel
Released only to those
Godly sworn to die,
Prostrate on altar high.

I Drank Of Nectar Or Was It Wine?

I tried yesterday
To fill a thought
Without you by my side,
Against the sun and after rain
Leaving dampened footsteps
Sure to stay awhile.

Yes, I live again the time we shared
Friday after math and soda,
Wandering down the avenue
Obscuring sense and what we saw.

I drank of nectar or was it wine?
Somehow given me that time.
All I know was the look you had
When first you offered,
Sure to stay awhile.

Sunday Afternoon

Does this mean you like me?
Fair across the straits
Of losing you
Repair of life to spend,
Time and pain to heal?

Your lingering nod
And grin for palpable tomorrows
The strain of speaking tête à tête
Across the jelly breakfast spills
Elbows of impatience sitting here
Waiting, wait-crowned maiden sipping
Red-rosed teas and tears of fallen
Drools of eyes and quiver of heart
How long to step there, here placed
Waving hands, we're here and that's all,
Still trapped on a Sunday afternoon.

And the cats roar across the empty time
Without human feel to brace the world
And sense to make life real
Alone, alone spanning earthen floor
Hurrying humans to fetch the locket
Of touch and softly spoken kiss.
Betrayal of not knowing the link
Or step sojourn to meet and breathe
The strength to adore and learn
Breaking the tissue of hesitancy
Still trapped on a Sunday afternoon.

Still Falls My Object Grace

Still falls my object grace,
Though she is tense from me
In bookly missions I admire,
I seek a cautious play
In her room and mental empire.

Ado in thoughts of her,
I close my eyes as ardor comes
For words and harmony inspire
Still, she does not move
Doom and darkness become dire.

Alas! Time becomes the ogre
As she remains aloof of my desire
The rhyme cannot go higher
The sun does set without avail
Disinterest and devil did conspire.

Lost Words Without Rhyme

What have you done to love
To shut the nights
From a caring soul
That bears the gift of faith?

Hardened thoughts you have
Can melt when met with truth,
Even with dimlit caress
Lost words without rhyme
And clumsy acts all for you.

What sorrow and wistful winds
Are there to counter age,
When plain it comes anew
To find and break asunder
Travail and tears that life does bring?

You Know

Is this the way
The softened blow
Sparing then the pain
To end the share of life
To say goodbye
There is no way,
You know.

"Desire is a mutual thing
Come seeping through the year,
A trickle of smoke
In the winter's day
Constricting then the heart
With tender words and play,"
She said,
You know.

"You came in a great big red
Puff of steam
Superwhelming me
And quiet soul I have,
Please understand,
I like you,
You know."

Season
of
Autumn

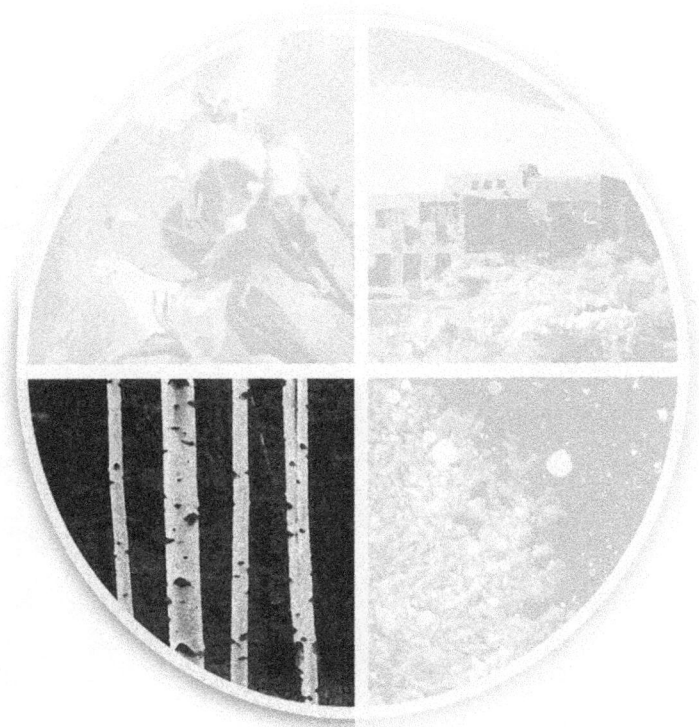

A Chiliad Of Soft Mornings

A chiliad of soft mornings
It would take
To kiss you one sweet time
And in those velvet seasons
There would be caress
Too many for a numbering scheme
Too few for an untold wish.

What I have is one grayish day
A tired world, caprice
The end of green and trees
Bracing for a hardened winter,
A glance stolen in the night
With darkened paths
Foreboding, fading
Like a half forgotten dream.

This Mortal Quest For You

My desire lives in the snow
And cold, all wintry bleak
And ice. Its fire is never dimmed
On the road to your near and far.

My desire lives in the sultry
And tortured time of summer,
Its shell laughing at the searing blows
While it makes its way to where you are.

My desire lives in the dead and dying
Far and dark and all askew
But its course never strays
As it follows my compass true.

My desire is all too vast
For dreary life to keep
Or nature's anger reroute
This mortal quest for you.

Stay With Me For Fear

Stay with me for fear
Of setting suns and dismal nights,
The haunting memories
And despair of little things,
A line or two of song,
A laugh in winter
And warmth in drizzly day.

Stay with me, I fear
An absence of comely hands,
A gift in midst
Of daily sorrow
Or a smile, done
Because there is so little time
For both a world and you.

She's Twenty-two Til June

She's twenty two til June
Sweetly smelling of lively fare.
She knows my heart and with it plays
All the more and makes me wait.

She's what I've held above
Dispelling all my fear and hate,
Young star and springlike moon,
This magic spell I cannot break.

I would tell her if I could
What temporal torture she does make.
My waiting, waiting turns to pall
She's twenty two and cruel.

My mind grows weary in my jail,
Impending doom, how long my jewel?
Not long to carry me in wood,
Waiting for the twenty four and mine.

It's Too Easy

It's too easy to hold you on sandy beach
And moonlit sea, its breezes embracing us
The sand too pliant and singing waves
All would chorus be to us.

Grassy meadow strolls make it easy
Midst the fragrance and stream flowing near
And distant trees green from nature's glory
Bids attesting to lovers' innocence.

Sunset knoll shows the reddened orb
Warming us hand in hand
Two shadows become one in the fading sun
Tranquillity immeasureable for courtship.

I want to hold you in the din and bleak
Cacophony, frigid air, cloudy skies,
Enchantment turning it from coarse and ugly
To earthly paradise.

The Shroud Of Evening

The shroud of evening
Is like a darkened lens
With light enough for memory
To harken when the need arises
As a snowfall, frost or chill
Requires the proper wrap
To stave the solitude.

In the mind your image
Stirs and snaps, awakening
From the dread a spirit
That sits next to me
And nudges me to fantasy.
How young we were
To think it would never change.

What I know now
From times we shared
Though pleasurable a tune,
Deep inside it stays.
We had roads ahead
Different ends in mind
Fortunes not quite the same.

Laughter And Sight Of You

We go on living,
Steps all in line;
A list we follow
Marking what we do
Lest we err in fate
And die in naught.

Laughter and sight of you
Brings the merit of it all
And the endless toil
Is small price to pay
That life allow the pause
And glory of the day.

Dangling In The Prime

It was a string
As if there were such
Dangling in the prime
And weakened by the wait
But made it mine to bear
Because it brought me back
To the goal it sought.

I asked her to read my eyes
As if she could
With so many things to do
Yet it was a place
When hiding was the course,
Swerving and safe to take
When feelings get in the way.

I followed the string
As it led me home
To rearrange my books
Gathering then the surge,
The will to seek again.
She will be there I know
With scent that draws the soul.

Into Slumber You Have Gone

Into slumber you have gone
In shadow my heart I have to keep.
Holding safely the future glee,
When she wakes and asks for me;
In words I have to write
This potion will join her to me.

She will arise when the words do say;
Her eyes bid farewell to sleep.
Together we aim to be
Everyone will plainly see
Monday mornings, mornings ever
I will call to thee.

For Someone Just Like Me

Running down the street
There's been a glimpse of her
In the crowds of dreary day;
I know she's looking
For someone just like me.

Tis sweet meeting you've going to make,
Never thinking, never finding
In running down the world,
When the magic will begin.

There is hope where there is aim
No need for errant face and miscast look;
There is spirit where there is sun
As it rises the die is cast;
The eyes betray the whispering call
When the halves will meet
Sending forth a life again.

Our Roller Coaster Affair

You said it was past the deadline
And there was no more time
To begin again after what was said,
Words we don't recall,
Thoughts we can't remember.

It was past
The rushed hour, rushed words
Pushed madly, racing last,
Hushed silence now; it's late.

The night has gone,
Unwinding reason and cooler heads,
Lonely times are sensed at *dawn;*
The mistake is met and we look
Down and find little to close and part.

The long day is gone,
Hopeless looks,
Smiles forgotten now;
All is done and found,
We wonder how
Our roller coaster affair
Had gotten off the track.

There Were Years

There were years
And words before the kiss
Senseless while the morn did pass
Congeal and long before we cared,
Moments torn from life with words
Before our hands did touch
Useless evermore.

A goodly span
Was lost, past the springlike day,
Past the place and things to do,
Found now and it's late.
Can all the loss be met today,
When countless words pale,
Before a sweet embrace.

Before The Sun And Aft

I want you now before we speak,
Before the rhyme and music.
Come to me before the walks,
Touches shared and empty words.

I want you now before the moon
Before the sun and aft.
See me now before polite,
Vain movements and all of that.

I want you now before the know
When desire is just as strong as now.
Let me kiss you hard before the said,
Wordless now and evermore.

I want you now before the snow
Whose coolness you will know
Will make my longing grow instead
Transcendent all the more.

The Times Do Not Call

The times do not call
You to come
And lift my head
With restful hands
And send a flow from them,
A grace and cure
For pains of days and woe
That break the soul.

The times do not call
For they are lonely times,
Stores of desolation
Mired with rusted wars
And ashen bones
Returning home.

The times do not call
And another life does end
A soul was spent
Before its blossomed fate.

The Little Things That Say Goodbye

It puts me to wonder
How busy you become
When the time to caress has come
To be shared under smiling moon,
And starlit skies til dawn.

You have other things to do
And friends to meet anew;
Silently, you creep away, hiding,
Friendly excuses,
Under indifferent eyes.
Shyly, you've walked away and done
The little things that say goodbye.

Don't Interrupt Me

Don't interrupt me in my manifest
Way of minding the hour without you.
Say what theme you will obey
In troubling my path to truth.

Don't interrupt the cyclic course
That leads to being true
For the days grow into miles
Far beyond your house so dear.

Where Are The Friendly Bowers?

Barren trees in wintry shadows,
Streets mirror solitude
Conversations that do not follow
Lapses come and go,
I see my pathway in dismay.

Where are the friendly bowers,
Roads to common gifts,
A place to be with you,
Converse with light persuasion?

You do not appear,
No responding eyes,
No tame caress nor scent of joy,
Seasons inclement
Uncertain to their end.

It Takes Too Long

Remember me in forest dreams,
The Fridays of yesteryear
When last we saw the ocean wave
Pulsing as the time went by.

It takes too long,
Impatient heart does call
To fleet the welcome
For a mastery of my soul.

Unshackle me with your bid,
Words to set me free
To sit idly by your side
And simply idolize.

Borne The Hours And Despair

Borne the hours and despair
The mental limbs do tire,
Bursting for the thought of you
A hunger that cannot wait.

Crave the rested self
That loosens time to hold you more
Strength to overcome the age
When we must part for other things.

I Can't Compete

I can't compete against the world
Of what may have been
The possible moments of the simple acts
Posing as undemanding time
Of you, restrained and aloof,
To know you up in stately court
And debut in maiden flair.

I can't say to you the pure
And innocent phrase
Of requisite nothing
Amidst a childlike glory you crave
And terms you hold dear
To hold you in abstract awe
And ponder when the time is here.

I can't be the one to turn
And divert you from somber mood
To be the one with ghastly smile
To speak of caring but wait awhile
For you to waken and sense my eyes
That have been long in promise
Taken in the heart and kept.

Remiss From Arms

She is mine in dream alone
Lent from absence
And fading time
Soon to know how far she is
Remiss from arms
Gentle in the day.

And now the dark will end
The sleep and her
And tranquil place
Soon to know how far she is
Remiss from arms
Gentle in the day.

Away From Me

Spying for her
Among the woods
Along the freshened songs
Of yesteryear
Held momentarily in the air
To remind this one of her.

She passes by
Hurrying toward the light
Away from me
Carrying the scent
I remember
Away from me.

Discomfort

How long do lonely days measure dreams
Discomfort, and nights to fill the time
Away from arms, disabling sleep
Strayed to be
To run to worlds of staying free
Rambling, tensile lives to flaunt
Committing steps to eternity?

The will to end this wait
Defying need for her
Arising yet again
The day will lead to her anew.

So Much Life Has Passed

So much life has passed
And now our souls do meet,
It is hard to be sane and quiet
While the memory stirs
And mixes real with fantasy.

It was a youthful force
That bore into the anxious mind
When the answer did not come
In time to form the bond
For rooted plans forever.

Your Letter Came

Your letter came and said to come,
There was a pause of memory
From long ago, of what could have been.
Youth's ardor and search for calm
But you had told me ⁄ I don't know.

There were days to undo the harm
And work was there to steer one's way
It is past the hour to ford the stream
Down the path too far,
The thread was severed in a dream.

We are far beyond where we were,
A world that's open'd my soul again.
There is no one yet that's sure
But a guarded search will find
The arms that speak of truth anon.

Season
of
Winter

Alone

Alone, a laugh that never leaves
A time with you
Imprinted
Gazing, enveloping the present
Senseless void today
As the foreign matter.

Until the longing day
Commits the pleasure of its end
And you appear
Waiting, lonely astride the dim
Where tired souls retreat and rest.

Avail, the night is cloudless
Impressed
With murmuring sounds
That steer toward freedom
Lest the void enisle you again.

Mortal Fools Who Lost

I lost her the week before.
Perhaps it was years and months
And still the days and more the hours
I can't remember how long ago.

Time is lost for me and yet
Today is always and the world's bent
To laugh at mortal fools who lost.

How sick is this reality,
Far from hills and far from shores
Where all cannot live with sanity,
I can't seem to make it go.

All the seasons and many more are sent
Reminding what was mine before;
It calls to me like the ocean's roar,
Lingering late, the winter pall is here.

Opposite The Setting Sun

What I can't do seems to be
The most important way
To hold you now. The kisses
I say are not heard above
Your thought far away
Like a dove in roving winds
Or a daydream in stuffy rooms.

What can I do, what sounds,
What binds to listen or feel
My yearning now?
The arms I held are gone,
Opposite the setting sun.
Your mind and heart are joining
Someone seen miles away
Gently, gently far from me.

Noon Is Gone

Noon is gone and she's not here
I haven't held her yet and felt
Her hand as it calms my jittery mind.
The day is passing and she's not near;
The sign does come and sits astride.
Other places, other thoughts bring to her
The time she has for someone else.

Her eyes will roam to worlds outside
My place and state of being
And dance sweet rhythms on foreign lands.
The hours pass and the day will end
Telling me she's gone to other climes
To share the noon and every sun
That sees me brightly left behind.

Moons Do Wane

The walls close in and moons do wane,
The weeks of ardor cool and time's disdain
The words are days and each a loss
Pursuing the endless trek of age
And crossing streams of lost.

The halls of time and moons do wane,
The walks of fondly fade and lost domain
The nights are ill und astray do pass
Stretching then the trials of days
And pressing thoughts of past.

The moons do go on and wails do fall,
The winds of barren flow and last disdain,
The years are here and steal the kiss
Trapping then the mount of moments,
And desire that kills.

The wails close in and moons do wane.

Dangling In The Time Passbook

A request for time
Leads me to more maybe's
And more meantimes
And I don't know's
That keep me spinning.

A stagger to hope
Wasting the hours
Of looking straightly
Just for consider
and letting the feel where it would.

I want to know the others
And join them in the maybe
Dangling in the time passbook
Turning leaves as you want,
Like painting your nails.

It's been too much of a season
My mind now only a shudder
From the burden of time
A lowering of ardor is sorrow
The parting a measure of loss.

Rule the Pented Sense

Rule the pented sense forgotten now
Fractured time to spend
I close my eyes, tearing then the daily song,
The noise masking memory without her
Slowly asking me where her presence?

The nights!
Perfidy of stars and moonlit crimes
To pain me more of vacuous wants
Vicious waits,
Plaintive seams of a lonely man.

She does not call, she does not come
To end...
Severing mine the vision of careless bliss.

How Long Do Loveless Days Measure Dreams?

How long do loveless days measure dreams?
Discomfort, and nights to fill the terror
Formed of losing her
Disably leaving me,
Awesomely strayed to be
To run to worlds, her whims do lead,
Do grant the hardened thoughts of staying free,
Rambling, tensile lives to flaunt, to want,
Away from committing steps to where?

The tears to end this wait
An inseparable rhyme
And crave, movement nowhere, nowhere
Sent again in sunrise.

The Anger Of Missing Her

The anger of missing her
Disquieting fear of never holding
Moments prompt with joy
————away from her
Distancing a look, a touch;
How far does this hour seem.

And comes the tiresome day
Of not seeing her again,
Again to wish the half embrace,
To rise and wake anxious hopes
And listen for her bound to me,
Softly next to me, whispering
Nonsense to pass the time.

When does she come,
Suddenly—wanted rest from lonely waits,
To crown the future days
With absent dream of losing her...

What Time Is Made To Miss

What time is made to miss
The happy days dreamed with you?
The casual walks, restless thoughts
Of seeing you in crowds,
Hearing you 1augh, your idle talk
Absent still, slipping times
To cross the humble hope still left,
Feebly yearning,
Cornering these embers alone to fade.

We Cheated Death and Gods

A cloud of absence
Unwraps my days,
I cannot think it through.

A wish to walk
And find someplace new,
Where we count the ways
We cheated death and gods
And intend to do so more.

I remember, yes, the dampened chill
Of missing you again,
There is no midway stroll,
No carving of the times,
Cotton candy that's unspun
I find there's no chance to start anew.

I Moved To Hold You Then

It was on the eve of May,
Settled airs and lively blossoms
I moved to hold you then,
Sunday's quiet and strolling pair
Along the edge to feelings' allure
But we missed the timely step.

In passing hours of waning strength,
Endless work and mindless leisure,
You didn't want the words to come;
Listless hours fuel the fear to fantasy,
Forsake the world that traps the time
And leaves us in a vacant prime.

For lack of touch, I craved you more
The anxious waits subdued me not
With memory of ardor past.
I owned the pain that loss does stir
For it only lasts until the sun appears
And parts quickly when you're here.

I Would See Forever

I would see forever
And you would say no
To be the end of dreams
Of spirit and earthly fires
That chase the fears
And breathe new life in me.

I could see you now
Between the mortal walls
Of oceans and deserts gray
And feel the pain of birth
And time that eats the soul
When you're not near.

I could see in clouds and mist
The end of dawns and sky
Where I would go and lose
The manner of seeing you.
Your glance now somewhere else,
Pursuing aims in worlds afar.

An Ocean Of Thoughts

An ocean of thoughts fill my mind
Waves repeating ancient promise
Of counting days like grains of sand
It was you I viewed long ago
Walking on the shore alone.

It was then in evening cool
Despite the noisy spray
I heard a soothing whisper
Like a hand upon my crown
A tide rising in my breast.

The words were said before
Yet never felt this way
Their reach beyond the mind
Like pages from a godly book
Leaping unto sleeping soul.

I come to sit and stare
Sometimes in gentle rain
Waves breaking eternally
The shore with no footsteps
A dream fools me once again.

About the Author

Andres C. Salazar spent decades on the east coast before returning as professor at the University of New Mexico in 2002. He earned a doctorate at Michigan State University and currently resides in Santa Fe, New Mexico. He is author of *Release from Cibola,* the first novel in a trilogy on the life of Reyes Cordova who grows up during the 1950s in Northern New Mexico within a disenfranchised and impoverished Spanish-speaking culture.

Readers Guide
An Interview with the Author

Q: Seasons categorizes poems into the phases of the year. Do you believe human love has four phases?

A: Certainly there are phases to love but I admit that some people would attribute fewer or more phases than four. My vote is for at least four. In the same way you could argue that the earth's rotation around the sun causes more than four seasons of the year. The point is that there are phases, how many is arguable.

Q: The poems in "Seasons" have settings or backgrounds, often playing a large role in establishing a mood for an amorous expression. Is love dependent on settings?

A: Many a romantic mood is enhanced by physical separation or the environment—candlelight, moon lit nights, etc. I don't think the "right" setting is essential for love to blossom. It is more a question of having other activities enhance or interfere with the feelings that lead to the attraction between two people. The sound of the words as well as their extended meaning and arrangement given an environment can yield new dimensions to the poetry of love.

Q: So much has been written about love. What motivated you to take on a subject where it is difficult to differentiate from its vast literature?

A: I agree that it is a challenge but it is an important topic, perhaps one that defines you first as a person and then how serious you are as an artist or writer. To ignore love is to give up on life. And I believe that there are thousands, millions perhaps, moods of love. The satisfaction that comes from writing about it is in finding a new way to describe the mood as it takes over you. Each mood is a unique blend of the active spiritual and physical forces within us when we are attracted to someone. Time is an important factor in the mood's realization because of human aging, experience and the fear of death. We all react differently to time and what we do becomes our unique signature.

Q: In "Seasons" the names of the ladies—Eve, Mary, Beatrice and so on—as well as their features—green eyes for example—are featured prominently as they are in the literature by other male authors. Are you referring to classical allusions or do they mean something else?

A: Certainly the names carry a legacy of meaning in religion, literature and human understanding. Eve can mean the mother, the beginning, or eternity just as much as Mary. They are abstract loves in a sense. What brings it back to mortality, to real life, to the sensual world is the reference to a woman's feature, the green eyes or brown hair, for example.

Q: In the book you make reference to love's role in the "mind" as well as to the part it plays in physical attraction. What separates the roles and is one more important than the other?

A: The literature tends to favor the mental role as the more lasting realization, the one that transcends any physical attraction that usually dominates at the beginning of an amorous relationship. The mind plays a bigger role in finding the soul mate which represents the ultimate goal in love.

Q: As one reads the poems it appears that different women are the targets of the amorous observations. Do you believe love to be monogamous or how does love manifest itself with different people being loved?

A: The word "love" can mean any one of the many aspects of affec‑ tion. Love of parents or friends is certainly different from its romantic version. Affection of the amorous kind can reach various levels with the partner we meet in our search for the soul mate, hence the different names. Having found the soul mate, monogamy or fidelity is the rule but not because of cultural pressure.

Q. Over what time period were these selected poems written? Was there any set of events that triggered them?

A: They were written over a span of many years. In that time I ob‑ served that the nature of amorous love changed with experience—not only with the inevitable ups and downs but also with age, temperament and social environment. In terms of events, every poet is moved with a significant personal happening and that evokes a literary response. I cannot say that any one type of event causes me to put pen to paper.

Q: Can we look forward to more books of poetry or are you concentrating on something else?

A: There is a book of poems in Spanish—*Siglos*. Unlike *Seasons* it has poems on various subjects but a few have a "love" theme. Novel writing takes up most of my literary time.

* 9 7 8 0 8 6 5 3 4 9 6 9 8 *